Little Quilts

All Through The House

That Patchwork Place®

Alice Berg

♡

Mary Ellen Von Holt

♡

Sylvia Johnson

Credits

Editor . . . . Ursula Reikes
Managing Editor . . . . Greg Sharp
Copy Editor . . . . Liz McGehee
Text and Cover Design . . . . . Joanne Lauterjung
Typesetting . . . . Joanne Lauterjung
Photography . . . . Brent Kane
                                                Dave Young
Illustration and Graphics . . . . Laurel Strand
                                                Barb Tourtillotte

That Patchwork Place, Inc., PO Box 118, Bothell, WA
98041-0118
USA

Printed in Hong Kong
98 97 96 95 94   6 5 4 3

Library of Congress Cataloging-in-Publication Data

Berg, Alice,
    Little quilts / Alice Berg, Sylvia Johnson, and Mary Ellen Von Holt.
        p.   cm.
    ISBN 1-56477-033-8 :
    1. Quilting—Patterns. 2. Patchwork—Patterns. 3. Miniature quilts. 4. Doll quilts. I. Johnson, Sylvia . II. Von Holt, Mary Ellen. III. Title.
TT835.B356 1993
746.9'7'0228—dc20   93-2611
                                        CIP

Dedication

We wish to dedicate this book to our supportive husbands and children, our quilting friends, and the many talented designers in our industry who led the way for us.

Acknowledgments

We wish to thank . . .

Janet Rawls and Jeannine Hartman—for their fine quilting

Barbara Butler and Janet Gardner—for the use of their Little Quilts

Susan Upchurch—for her invaluable computer expertise

Kathy Gist—for her proofreading assistance

Our "Friday Stitch-In" group

The East Cobb Quilters' Guild

Loren and Barbara Rozeboom, Charlie and Karin Snyder—for the use of their wonderful homes

Dave Young, Design and Visual Effects, Atlanta, Georgia—for room photography

North American Bear Co., Inc., Chicago, Illinois

TABLE OF CONTENTS

Welcome to the wonderful world of Little Quilts®! We are thrilled to have been invited by That Patchwork Place to write this book and to work with their talented, dedicated staff.

We would like you to get to know us and how we got our start, learn to make Little Quilts, then have fun using them throughout your home. Take our home tour and see how these quilts add instant warmth to any setting. Let us show you our techniques and how we use fabric in a magical way to create charming doll-size quilts.

If you are a beginner, these projects are a great way to learn before you plunge into that king-size quilt you had in mind. For those of you with several notches in your thimble, these quilts make great gifts for all the friends and relatives who have added their name to your "make-me-a-quilt" list.

Have fun making Little Quilts and don't worry about perfection! If the seams don't match up and the appliqué stitches show, give the quilt a strong tea bath and tell your friends, "Look at this old doll quilt I made when I was ten years old; we found it in the attic!" Aging the finished quilt in a tea bath may seem hard to do, but it is definitely better than a friend's suggestion that we take Little Quilts to a day-care center and leave them for six months. That would age them for sure!

We hope you enjoy your visit with Little Quilts. Take off your shoes and stay awhile, and come back often.

The creators and designers of Little Quilts, which is located in Marietta, Georgia. Seated, from left to right: Sylvia Johnson, Alice Berg, and Mary Ellen Von Holt.

Little Quilts partners, Alice Berg, Sylvia Johnson, and Mary Ellen Von Holt, work as a team, combining special skills and talents where needed to produce The Little Quilt Collection of Patterns, The Little Quilt Kit Collection, and the pattern booklets: *American Crib Quilts—Inspirations from the 19th Century*. Little Quilts patterns, kits, and accessories are sold worldwide, providing magazines and other publications with small projects for beginners. In addition, Little Quilts has sponsored awards for small quilt categories in various quilt shows and contests across the country.

Having taught successfully at quilt symposiums and the International Quilt Festival in Houston, Texas, Alice, Sylvia, and Mary Ellen bring a simple, creative idea on a smaller scale to the quiltmaker of today. They like to call Little Quilts "dessert for the quilter."

Originally from south Florida, Alice has been involved in quilting since 1976. Patchwork is her focus and she is currently working on a series of folk medallion quilts. In 1992, she was the grand prize winner of the Celebrate America Quilt Contest, sponsored by *Country Home* magazine. She has exhibited her work at the International Quilt Market in Houston, Texas, and in various regional shows and quilt publications. Alice is an "idea" person, with something always cooking in her head, and is known for taking a theme and carrying it as far as it will go. She and her husband, Wally, have three sons in college.

Sylvia was born and raised in Georgia, a true Southerner! She was a kindergarten teacher prior to raising two sons. Her love for traditional American needlework brought quilting into her life. She enjoys making quilts to commemorate special occasions, such as parents' anniversaries, children's graduations, and friends' accomplishments. Sylvia collects needlework samplers and antique quilts, with a special interest in quilts of the 1930s. Keeping records for the business falls into her lap, and often, she is the "stabilizer." Sylvia and her husband, Butch, are active in Scouting and share a love of the outdoors.

Mary Ellen has been quilting for over fifteen years and is interested in whatever is going on. Challenge quilt projects have become a specialty. She is the "contemporary quilter" of the three and creates innovative patchwork quilts with machine quilting. Mary Ellen has a background in art and advertising and is skilled at fabric coordination. She teaches classes on creating traditional scrap quilts and is known as the "Rotary Cutting Queen" in the area. "Production & Art" is how the sign reads on her office door. She and her husband, Ron, have a son in college and a daughter in high school. They moved to the Atlanta area from Chicago in 1981.

Alice, Sylvia, and Mary Ellen are active in their local quilt guild, serving as officers and chairwomen, and teaching classes in area quilt shops. It has always been important for them to help promote their love for quiltmaking in their community, as well as fulfilling other personal interests. They credit "compromise" as the key ingredient to their success, along with supportive families and friends.

LITTLE QUILTS
AND HOW THEY GREW

In the early 1980s, American country decorating was growing in popularity. Many magazines and publications began to appear, showing cozy, inviting rooms filled with collections and furnishings of earlier times. As we turned the pages and dreamed of living in such settings, we began to notice small quilts used in a variety of ways and how they gave a softness to the other hard, primitive pieces. Trying to purchase a small quilt like the ones shown was difficult, not to mention costly, if you were lucky enough to find one. As quilters, we decided to make our own.

Our first few attempts were not very successful. The quilts looked too new! Experiments using fabric from clothing at the thrift store and various overdyeing techniques (including a recipe involving chewing tobacco) still did not provide the necessary ingredients. Finally, we achieved a look we had been searching for and it had been right in front of us. We noted the following points as the process evolved.

- ❤ Make them like a regular quilt but scale them down to a small size.
- ❤ Use fabrics on hand, slightly uncoordinated and scrappy, and combine with thin quilt batting.
- ❤ Use simple quilting and tea dye to produce an "aged" look.
- ❤ When completed, press the quilts flat and let the decorating fun begin.

Making the quilts became an obsession, and the idea of selling them entered our minds. We talked our way into a popular local antique show and started sewing. We invited other friends to join. Ninety-five Little Quilts were sold within a few hours. As we continued to sell the quilts, people began to collect them. We also noticed many admirers wanted to make their own but often were not confident in their fabric selection, so we began making kits, complete with everything but a needle, thread, and time. Word spread and so did the kit business. With $47.00 each and fabric from our collections, work began in Alice's basement, later moving to Mary Ellen's, and now residing in offices in Marietta, Georgia, outside Atlanta. A great staff assists us, and with an office full of women, we have gained the reputation of "We know everything—or at least have an opinion on everything." A simple "museum" displays early kits and patterns with handwritten headers and early fabrics as a reminder of those first days in business. Since 1986, Little Quilts has enjoyed continued growth and success. To women with a creative idea and a desire to go into business, we offer this advice—"Watch out, you're going to do great!"

A LITTLE QUILT IS . . .

A small, not miniature, quilt based on a traditional design. It is made just like a large quilt, consisting of quilt blocks, borders, binding, and hand quilting. The pieces are easy to manage, and you can use various construction techniques. It is a wonderful "happy" for quilters to share with friends and family for all occasions. Beginning quiltmakers experience the thrill of completing a project, which is like eating chocolate candy—you want more!

Blocks: 5" (average size)
Sashing strip width: 1"
Border width: 2" to 4"
Binding width: ¼"
Quilt sizes: 9" to 30" (average size)

You will need only simple, basic supplies to make a Little Quilt. You can use machine piecing for most projects, along with hand appliqué and traditional hand piecing. Use any quick-piecing and -cutting techniques you choose. A few of our favorites are included in the General Directions.

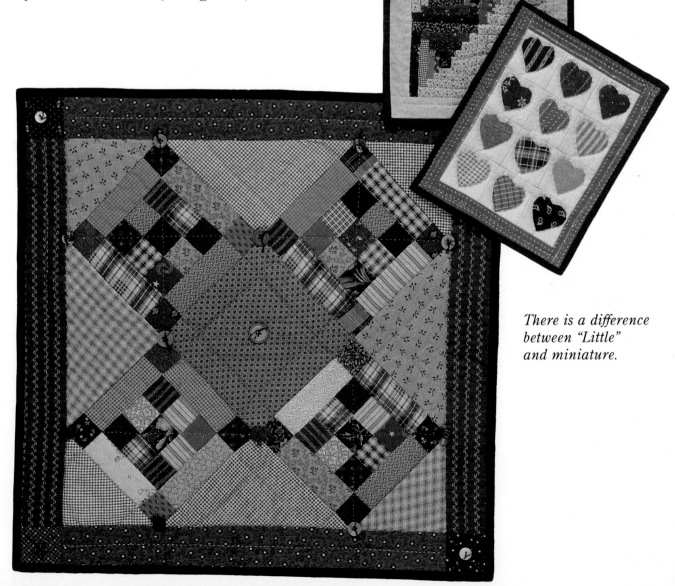

There is a difference between "Little" and miniature.

Antique Quilt Blocks

Using odds and ends of antique quilt blocks, combined with carefully selected new fabric, is an effective way to create Little Quilts with a primitive, authentic look.

When shopping antique shows and flea markets, ask vendors for old quilt blocks. They often are surprised that anyone would be interested. Choose blocks that are smaller in scale and "scrappy." Blocks that work well are Four Patch and Ninepatch, triangles, and Log Cabin; however, wonderful surprises happen with almost any block.

Take your collection of old blocks and shuffle them around into workable arrangements. Remember that you are making a small doll-size quilt and that blocks can be cut into smaller pieces. Sew the parts together—don't worry about seams matching! Add any borders if desired, then press. Layer with very thin batting and quilt a simple design, using tan or black quilting thread. Bind the quilt, tea dye, and when dry, press flat. Bravo!

To help you achieve the Little Quilt look, we'd like to share a secret that will ensure successful results. We call certain fabric colors and designs "magic" because when added to most projects, they give an "aged" look. These "magic" fabrics create an interesting quilt full of surprises. When we teach classes, we provide each student with a packet of these fabrics. Although many of the colors are new and sometimes uncomfortable to use, they give the quiltmaker new freedom with color and fabric. Make "magic" fabrics a part of all your quiltmaking. Listen to the applause!

Black—prints, plaids, fabrics with black in them

Plaids and Stripes—all types

Bubble Gum Pink—a "thirties" pink known by various names

Purples—prints and small geometrics

Browns—shades such as cinnamon and dark brown

Mustard Golds—several different prints

Tan—"nothing" prints (tan on light-background designs)

A sampling of "magic" fabrics

Magic fabrics are mixed with other selections.

The Design Wall

Having a design wall is invaluable when constructing a quilt of any size, especially a Little Quilt. This wall will enable you to stand back, position blocks, and audition borders for your project. Place the quilt parts on the wall and sew them together when you are happy with the arrangement. A reducing glass, which is the reverse of a magnifying glass, helps you look at your quilt from a distance. You can buy one at your quilt shop or art supply store.

To make your own design wall, purchase a 1½-yard piece of flannel or fleece. Tack or tape the fleece to a wall. If you do not have a spare wall, cover a large piece of plywood or foam core (from the art supply store). You can easily store this board when it is not in use.

A design wall and reducing glass are a quilt designer's best friends!

These Little Quilts are easy to make, and we want you to have a good time making them. You will find instructions for rotary cutting and machine piecing. Templates are provided on pages 73–79 if you wish to use more traditional methods to make the blocks. If you use rotary-cutting methods, you can compare your rotary-cut pieces to the templates to check for accuracy. All measurements include ¼"-wide seam allowances, unless otherwise specified.

ROTARY CUTTING

You can use a rotary cutter, acrylic ruler, and mat to accurately cut several layers of fabric at one time. These tools are invaluable when making multi-fabric quilts. Use the rotary cutter to cut strips for many of the projects in this book. The Bias Square® is especially useful for squaring up blocks in Little Quilts.

For rotary-cutting techniques, consult *Shortcuts: A Concise Guide to Rotary Cutting* by Donna Lynn Thomas, a That Patchwork Place book.

MACHINE PIECING

Often, what we think is a ¼" seam can be too large or small. Any variation in your ¼"-wide seam allowance will affect the size of your block. Use a ruler or template plastic with a ¼" grid to check this measurement on your machine and determine a guide for your sewing. Place a piece of masking tape on the plate of the machine to mark your "spot." Change your needle frequently, and use 10–12 stitches per inch. Backstitching is not necessary, since seams will cross each other. Chain piecing saves time and thread.

For machine-piecing techniques, consult *A Perfect Match: A Guide to Precise Machine Piecing* by Donna Lynn Thomas, a That Patchwork Place book.

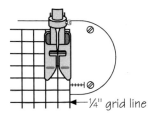
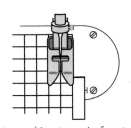

Use ¼" or ⅛" graph paper to locate a new seam guide.

Put masking tape in front of needle along edge of graph paper to guide fabric.

Little Lesson

To check your ¼"-wide seam allowances, sew three 1½"-wide strips together. Press. Measure the width of the center strip. It should measure 1".

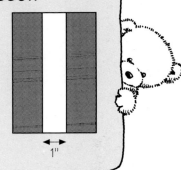

PRESSING

It is important to press seams as you sew them. This helps with matching seams and helps to ensure that the finished block will be the correct size. Pull your ironing board up close to your machine. If you need the exercise, place it across the room so you are forced to move!

After sewing strips together by machine, press the seams while they are closed before pressing them to one side. This will relax the stitching and keep the strips from waving. Press seams in one direction, toward the darker fabric.

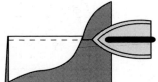

Press seam after sewing, before pressing one way or the other.

Press strips open by opening the pieces with the iron.

13

APPLIQUÉ

Templates for appliqué pieces do not include seam allowances. Draw around the template on the right side of the fabric. Cut ⅛" to ¼" away from this line. Turn under the seam allowance and finger press. Run a row of basting close to the edge to hold the seam allowance in place. Clip only when necessary. Pin the pieces in place, noting where one piece may overlap another. A seam allowance that is overlapped by another piece need not be basted under. Overlapped areas on pattern pieces are indicated with a dotted line. Using a single thread to match the appliqué piece, sew the piece in place with an appliqué stitch. A running stitch will appear on the back.

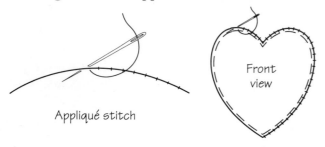

Appliqué stitch

Front view

Needle turning is another method and works well for simple shapes, such as hearts. Baste the shape to the background fabric about ⅛" inside the drawn line. Use the needle to turn the seam allowance under as you sew around the appliqué.

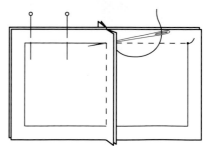

Back view

A quick way to appliqué pieces is to use fusible webbing. Follow manufacturer's directions given with the product. No seam allowance is needed when using this method. Use a buttonhole or blanket stitch to finish edges, either by hand or machine if your machine has the capability.

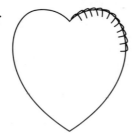

HAND PIECING

Hand piecing is a traditional method that can be enjoyed anytime and anywhere. While it may not be a speedy method, it can be very relaxing and enjoyable. You can easily keep a small bag of hand piecing to do while traveling or while waiting at the dentist's office.

For hand piecing, cut templates from plastic, using the dashed lines marked on the inside of the templates. Using a sharp pencil, trace around the template on the wrong side of the fabric, paying attention to grain lines in the fabric as indicated on the pattern. This drawn line is the actual sewing line. Cut ¼" beyond this line to add the seam allowance. Lay out the pieces, right side up, so you can see the design. You will sew small units together to make larger ones. Follow the piecing diagrams. This is like sewing a puzzle—accuracy is a must. Pin pieces together, matching seam lines. Sew on the lines, using a small running stitch; check to make sure you are stitching on the lines of both pieces. Only sew on the lines—seam allowances must remain free.

Trim seams to ⅛" after sewing each one. When block is complete, press well.

Little Lesson

Pin your patchwork and appliqué pieces to a square of muslin to keep them in order for hand sewing.

QUILTING

Mark quilting lines lightly with an ordinary pencil, washable fabric marker, or white pencil. Masking tape in different widths is also helpful. Cut backing and batting a few inches larger than the quilt top all the way around. Layer backing, batting, and quilt top. Baste the layers together.

Tie a single knot in the end of an 18" length of quilting thread. Insert the needle in the top layer of the quilt about ½" from where you want to start quilting. Slide the needle through the batting and bring the needle out on the marked quilting line. Gently tug on the thread until the knot pops through the fabric, burying the knot in the batting. Make small, even stitches through all layers, following your marked quilting lines. To end your stitches, make a single knot about ¼" from the quilt top and tug on the knot until it pops into the batting. Bring the needle out ½" away from your last stitch and clip the thread.

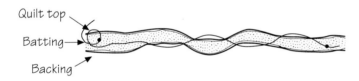

Quilt top
Batting
Backing

Quilt from the center out and use a hoop when you can. Quilting will reduce the size of your quilt slightly.

Complete quilting instructions can be found in *Loving Stitches: A Guide to Fine Quilting* by Jeana Kimball, a That Patchwork Place book.

BINDING

Trim away excess batting and backing fabric. Cut 1½"-wide strips across the width of the fabric (crosswise grain). You can also use strips from your basket. Join enough strips to go around the quilt, plus 4"–5". Place binding on the quilt top, with right sides together and raw edges even. Fold ½" of the binding back and pin. Place pins along one side at a time and sew through all layers, using a ¼"-wide seam. Stop stitching ¼" from the corner, backstitch, clip threads, and remove from machine. Fold the binding straight

up, then bring it straight down. Stitch from the edge as shown. Repeat for each corner. When you reach the starting point, sew the end across the beginning fold. Cut off excess binding. Bring the raw edge over to the back, fold under ¼", and blindstitch in place, covering the machine stitching. Tuck corners to form a miter.

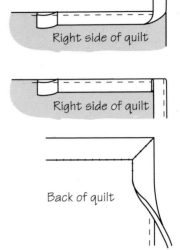

Right side of quilt

Right side of quilt

Back of quilt

TEA DYEING

Use a tea bath to help "age" your quilt. When you finish the quilt, place it in the tea solution. This makes for a nervous moment, but we haven't seen a Little Quilt yet that didn't benefit from this "aging" process.

Our Tea Dyeing Recipe

1 large bowl
2 quarts *hot* tap water
6 to 8 tea bags

Steep tea bags in hot water for 15 minutes. Remove tea bags. Add quilt and soak in the tea solution 15 to 30 minutes. Rinse in cool water. Squeeze out excess water. Lay flat to dry. Press the quilt to reshape.

LABELING YOUR LITTLE QUILT

Make a Little Quilt label for your finished quilt. Cut a piece of muslin approximately 3" x 5" and iron onto the shiny side of a piece of freezer paper to provide a firm surface for writing. Place the muslin piece over the label (shown below) and carefully trace, using a fine-point permanent pen. Use a pen with a contrasting ink color for filling in the information, if desired. Remove the freezer paper after you've finished writing the information on the label. Trim excess muslin. Turn under a ¼"-wide seam allowance and carefully stitch to the back of the quilt, making sure your needle does not go through to the front.

EMBELLISHMENTS

We've used old buttons in several of our quilts. We sewed on the buttons with three strands of embroidery floss and scattered them randomly over the quilt. We've also used the buttonhole stitch in several of our quilts. Use a sharp embroidery needle and two strands of black floss, about 20" long. Begin with a knot on the back and end by weaving a small amount of thread in previous stitches on the back to secure the end. Working from left to right, bring the needle out at the edge of the piece. Take an upright stitch to the right with the needle pointed down, keeping the thread under the needle, and come out on the edge. Turn the corner as illustrated.

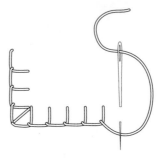

Buttonhole stitch

You can do this stitch or a similar one with some sewing machines, using a blind hem, overcast, or blanket stitch.

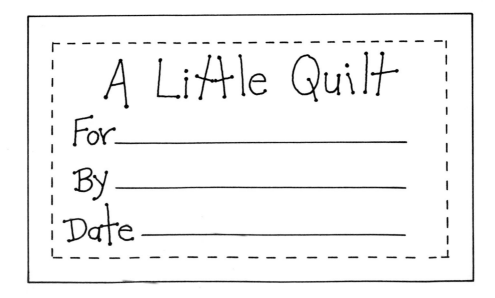

It's always nice to know some "tricks of the trade," and we include the methods we use to construct certain blocks here to help you, too. This is where you will begin to see the value of your precut strips!

HALF-SQUARE TRIANGLE BLOCKS

Rotary cutting and machine piecing make these a snap. Determine the finished size of the short side of the triangle needed. Add $\frac{7}{8}$" to this measurement. Cut a square this size, then cut once diagonally to yield two triangles. Sew pairs of triangles together to make a half-square triangle block. If you have extra triangles from previous projects, you can cut them to size, using the Bias Square® from That Patchwork Place.

SIMPLE FOUR PATCH BLOCKS

Using fabrics from your basket of 1½"-wide strips, sew pieces together in pairs, using many short strips for variety. Cut the sewn strips into 1½"-wide pieces. Join two pieces to form the Four Patch block.

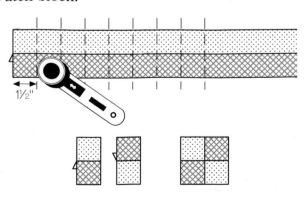

1½"

SCRAPPY NINEPATCH BLOCKS

Using fabrics from your basket of 1½"-wide strips, sew pieces together in pairs, using many short strips for variety. Press seams while still closed; then press seam to one side. Add a third strip. Crosscut strips into 1½" pieces. Sew three pieces together to make a Ninepatch, making sure to match seams between blocks. Ignore seam direction if necessary. Don't worry about matching fabrics—be surprised!

For controlled-color Ninepatch blocks:

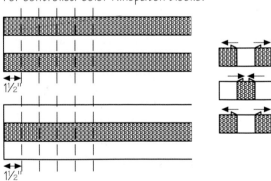

1½"

1½"

For random-color Ninepatch blocks:

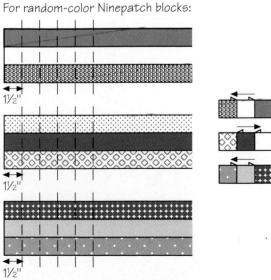

1½"

1½"

1½"

SHORTCUT STARS

Scrap stars are easy to make, using fabrics from your basket of 1¾"-wide strips and 3" squares. For each star, you will need:

1 square, 3" x 3", for the center
8 dark squares, each 1¾" x 1¾", for star points
4 light squares, each 1¾" x 1¾", for background corners
4 light rectangles, each 1¾" x 3", for background of star points

1. Draw a diagonal line from corner to corner on the wrong side of the star point squares.
2. Place one of these squares on one end of the rectangle as shown below. Sew on the marked line. Trim the corner of the triangle, leaving a small seam allowance. Do not trim the rectangle corner. Press the triangle to the corner.
3. Place a second square on the opposite end of the rectangle, with the marked line as shown. Sew, trim, and press. Make four of these units.
4. Assemble the star as shown in the piecing diagram.

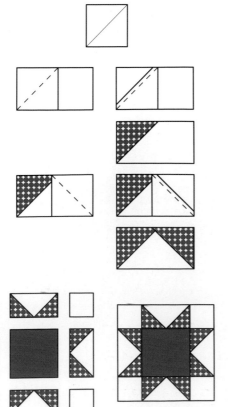

LOG CABIN CONSTRUCTION

Our favorite method for making Log Cabin blocks is familiar and simple. Build Log Cabin blocks individually to create a great scrap look. Select fabrics from your basket of 1¼"-wide strips.

   Note
A variety of center squares and arrangements are used in these projects. Check individual quilt directions.

1. Select a light strip and sew it to the center square. Trim the edges of the strip and press the seam away from the center square.
2. With the right side up, turn the block so that the last strip sewn is at the top. Sew a second light strip as shown and press the seam toward the outside (or away from center).

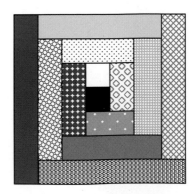

3. Add two dark strips in the same manner. Continue adding light and dark strips until the block has three rows of light strips and three rows of dark strips as shown.

HOUSES FROM STRIPS

From assorted 1½"-wide strips, rotary cut the following for each house:

- 5 squares, each 1½"x 1½", for sky between chimneys, and on either side of roof
- 2 squares, each 1½" x 1½", for chimneys
- 2 squares, each 1½" x 1½", for house
- 1 square, 1½" x 1½", for window
- 1 rectangle, 1½" x 5½", for house
- 1 rectangle, 1½" x 5½", for roof
- 1 rectangle, 1½" x 3½", for house
- 1 rectangle, 1½" x 2½", for door
- 1 rectangle, 1½" x 2½", for house

1. Draw a diagonal line on the wrong side of two of the 1½" x 1½" squares for the sky. Place 1 square on one end of the 1½" x 5½" rectangle for the roof as shown at right. Sew on the diagonal line. Trim the corner of the square, leaving a small seam allowance. Do not trim the rectangle corner. Press the triangle to the corner. Repeat with the other 1½" x 1½" square on the other end of the rectangle. There will be space between the triangles after they are sewn.

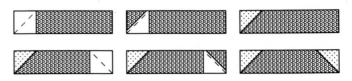

2. Assemble House block as shown in the piecing diagram.

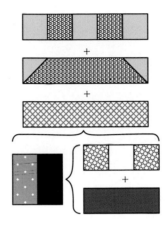 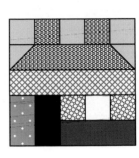

The Blocks

The quilt projects in this book use a collection of simple, traditional blocks. Hand or machine piecing may be used. Templates are provided for each piece in the pattern section.

Four Patch
Finished Block Size: 2"
1½"-wide strips
Template D

Half-Square Triangle
Finished Block Size: 2"
Template N

Ninepatch
Finished Block Size: 3"
1½"-wide strips
Template D

Large Heart
Finished Block Size: 3½"
Background square
(Template C)
Heart (Template A)

Small Heart
Finished Block Size: 3½"
Background square
(Template C)
Heart (Template B)

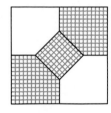

Bow Tie
Finished Block Size: 4"
Templates BB and CC

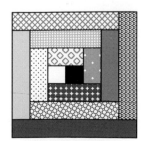

Log Cabin
Finished Block Size: 5¼"
1¼"-wide strips
Templates O, P, Q, R, S, T, U

Framed Ninepatch
Finished Block Size: 5"
1 Ninepatch block
Templates D, F

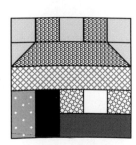

House
Finished Block Size: 5"
1½"-wide strips
Templates D, E, F, G, H, I

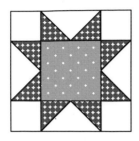

Star Block
Finished Block Size: 5"
1¾"-wide strips
Templates J, K, L, M

Sunbonnet Sue
Finished Block Size: 5"
Background square
(Template AA)
Sue (Templates 1, 2, 3, 4, 5, 6)

Overall Bill
Finished Block Size: 5"
Background square
(Template AA)
Bill (Templates 1, 2, 3, 4, 5, 6, 7)

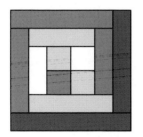
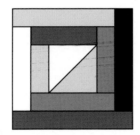

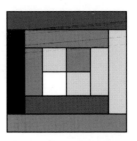
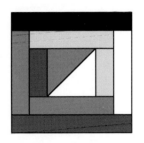

Log Cabin with Four Patch
or Half-Square Triangle Center
Finished Block Size: 5"
1¼"-wide strips
Templates V, W, X, Y, Z
Four Patch, 1½"-wide strips (Template D)
Half-Square Triangle (Template N)

Courthouse Steps with Four Patch
or Half-Square Triangle Center
Finished Block Size: 5"
1¼"-wide strips
Templates V, X, Z
Four Patch, 1½"-wide strips (Template D)
Half-Square Triangle (Template N)

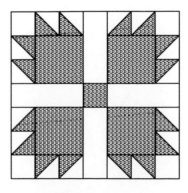

Wreath
Finished Block Size: 7"
Background square (Template EE)
Wreath (Templates 1, 2, 3, 4)

Bear's Paw
Finished Block Size: 7"
Templates D, F, I, HH

Little Quilts on Display

Making the quilts is only part of the fun! There are so many ways to use your Little Quilt, and we hope that by looking at the rooms we have photographed (pages 23–29), you will truly understand the versatility of these quilts.

Think of your Little Quilt as a textile painting. Place it in a grouping with a collection of other objects, such as baskets, shelves, and folk art. Fabrics used in the quilts do not need to match room furnishings exactly; a certain charm comes from mismatching. The softness of a quilt is instant success in decorating, no matter what your style.

HANGING LITTLE QUILTS

Use any of the following methods to hang your quilt.

- Attach two small safety pins to the back of the quilt, close to the top; then hang on tiny nails, like a picture.
- Use straight pins, which can be pushed through the corners of the quilt into the wall (depending on wall surface).
- Sew small rings to the back of the quilt; then hang on tiny nails.
- Attach a fabric "sleeve" and insert a strip of lattice with holes in it for hanging on small nails.
- Frame your Little Quilt.

You'll find so many ways to display your Little Quilt. Move them around and group colors for certain holidays. Enjoy your Little Quilt all through the house!

For the holidays! In a gather ___ ___ ice for friends and quilts, everyone feels at home. On the stairway wall: Homecoming ___ ___ ath, *top left*; Sunbonnet Sue Sampler, *top right*; Country Christmas, *bottom*. A Cinnamo ___ ___ arts quilt sits under the bear while Stars in the Snow *and* Country Garden Heart acce ___ ___ he chest of drawers. Two Celebration Flags *and a* Country Cabin *decorate the table;* Feed Sack Furrows *variation hangs from the island behind the chair.*

Your Little Quilt

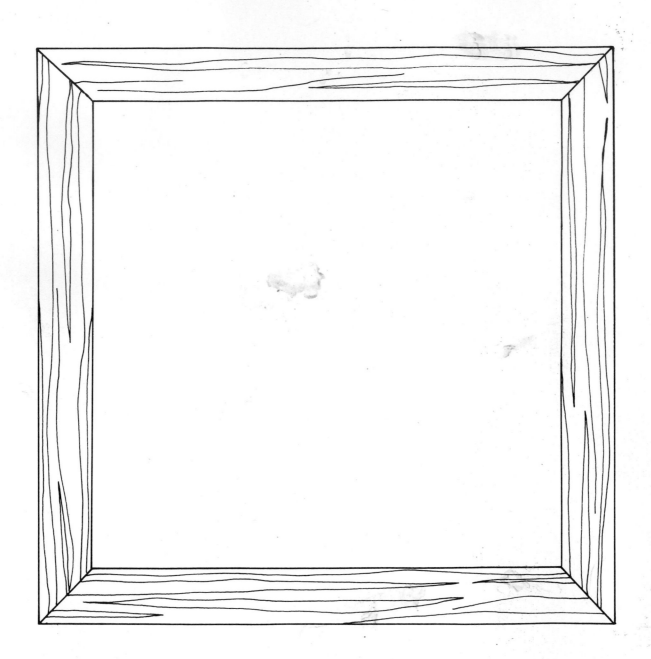

Now that you have seen how we make Little Quilts, perhaps you would like to design your own! Take any of the blocks from the book and combine them into your own creation. Take a photo of your "designer original" and paste it here.

A Little Quilt

For _____

By _____

Date _____

These Little Quilts are easy to make and we want you to have a good time making them. Instructions are for rotary cutting and machine piecing. If you wish to use more traditional methods to make the blocks, you will find templates on pages 73–79. If you use rotary-cutting methods, you can compare your rotary-cut pieces to the templates to check for accuracy. All measurements include a ¼"-wide seam allowance, unless otherwise specified.

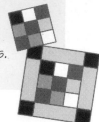

NINEPATCHES

The Ninepatch is a simple design with never-ending possibilities.
Use this block to make authentic-looking doll quilts.

Hopscotch

Quilt Size: 17½" x 17½"

Hopscotch *by Little Quilts, 1991, Marietta, Georgia, 17½" x 17½". Perfect on a table, this quilt, made in muted colors and embellished with buttons, is a decorating favorite. (Collection of Little Quilts)*

Framed Ninepatch Block
Finished Block Size: 5"
1½"-wide strips
Templates: D, F

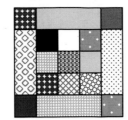

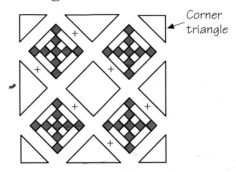

Materials
44"-wide fabric

Assorted fabric strips, each 1½" wide
Assorted prints for side triangles, center square, and corner squares, each approximately 8" x 8"
⅓ yd. border fabric
⅛ yd. binding
⅝ yd. backing
17 assorted buttons

Block Cutting and Assembly

1. Use an assortment of 1½"-wide strips to make 4 Ninepatch blocks as shown on page 17.
2. Frame the Ninepatch blocks. From assorted 1½"-wide strips, cut:
   16 strips, each 1½" x 3½"
   16 squares, each 1½" x 1½"
3. Sew 1½" x 3½" strips to opposite sides of a Ninepatch block. Sew a 1½" x 1½" square to each end of the remaining 1½" x 3½" strips and attach to the top and bottom of the block as shown.

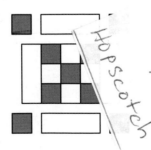

Quilt Top Assembly

1. From fabric for center square, cut 1 square, 5½" x 5½".
2. From 4 different fabrics, cut 1 square, 8¼" x 8¼"; cut twice diagonally to yield 4 side triangles (Template II).
3. From 4 different fabrics, cut 2 squares, each 5⅞" x 5⅞"; cut once diagonally to yield 4 corner triangles (Template JJ).
4. Arrange the blocks and side triangles as shown on this page. Sew the blocks and triangles together in diagonal rows as shown. Press the seams of alternating rows in opposite directions.

5. Sew the rows together, making sure to match the seams between each block. Add the corner triangles last.

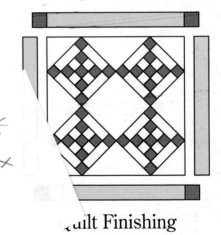

Corner triangle

6. From border fabric, cut 4 strips, each 2" x 14½". Sew 2 border strips to the sides of the quilt top.
7. From 4 different fabrics, cut 4 squares, each 2" x 2", for border corners. Sew a square to each end of the remaining border strips, then sew to top and bottom of quilt top.

Quilt Finishing

1. Layer the quilt top with batting and backing; baste.
2. Quilt as desired.

> **Suggestion**
>
> Quilt in-the-ditch around the Framed Ninepatch blocks and diagonally through the center. Outline the setting triangles with 1" lines. Quilt a single row ¾" from the border seam.

3. Bind the edges of the quilt.
4. Tea dye if desired.
5. Press the quilt.
6. Embellish with assorted buttons.

Let's Have a Picnic

Quilt Size: 24½" x 24½"

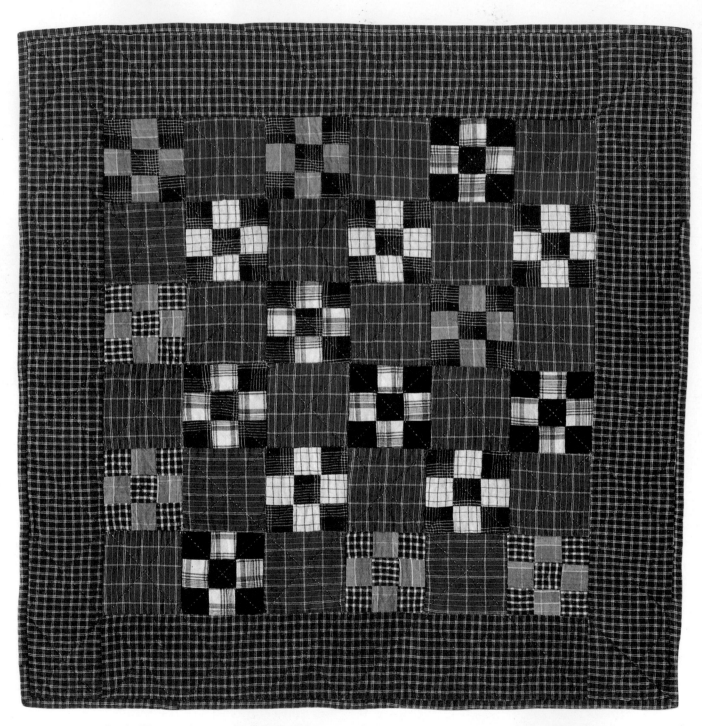

Let's Have a Picnic *by Sylvia Johnson, 1991, Marietta, Georgia, 24½" x 24½".*
Celebrate those patriotic days by using this quilt with your collection of Americana—it's
perfect in a basket on a sunny day! (Collection of Sylvia Johnson)

Ninepatch Block
Finished Block Size: 3"
1½"-wide strips
Template: D

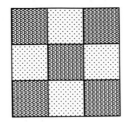

3. From border fabric, cut 2 strips, each 3½" x 18½", and sew to the sides of the quilt top. Cut 2 strips, each 3½" x 24½", and sew to the top and bottom edges of the quilt top.

Materials
44"-wide fabric

This project includes a variety of fabrics in a controlled color scheme.
Assorted red, white, and blue fabric strips, each 1½" wide
¼ yd. blue
⅝ yd. border and binding
¾ yd. backing

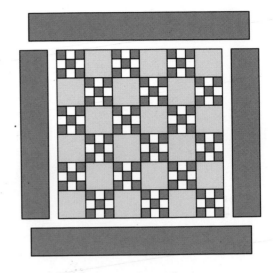

Block Cutting and Assembly

1. Use an assortment of 1½"-wide strips to make 18 Ninepatch blocks as shown on page 17.
2. From blue fabric, cut 18 squares, each 3½" x 3½" (Template FF).

Quilt Top Assembly

1. Sew blocks into rows, alternating Ninepatch blocks and blue squares as shown in the quilt plan on this page. Press the seams of alternating rows in opposite directions.
2. Sew rows together, making sure to match the seams between each block.

Quilt Finishing

1. Layer the quilt top with batting and backing; baste.
2. Quilt as desired.

Suggestion
Quilt diagonally across the center of the blocks and out onto the border.

3. Bind the edges of the quilt.
4. Tea dye if desired.
5. Press the quilt.

HOUSES

You can easily make these houses with fabric from your basket of 1½"-wide strips. Soon you will have a whole neighborhood.

Playhouses

Quilt Size: 20½" x 31½"

Playhouses *by Little Quilts, 1993, Marietta, Georgia, 20½" x 31½". Little houses all in a row! Using bright pastel fabrics from the strip basket, you can build this neighborhood quickly. (Collection of Little Quilts)*

House Block
Finished Block Size: 5"
1½"-wide strips
Templates: D, E, F, G, H, I

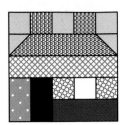

Assorted pastel fabric strips, each 1½"
    wide
3 different green strips, each 2" x 15½"
½ yd. border
¼ yd. binding
1 yd. backing

Block Assembly

Use an assortment of 1½"-wide strips to make 12 houses as shown on page 19.

Quilt Top Assembly

1. Sew blocks into 4 rows of 3 blocks each.
2. Join the rows, using a 2" x 15½" green strip as shown below.
3. From border fabric, cut 2 strips, each 3" x 25", and sew to the sides of the quilt top. Cut 2 strips, each 3" x 20½", and sew to the top and bottom of the quilt top.

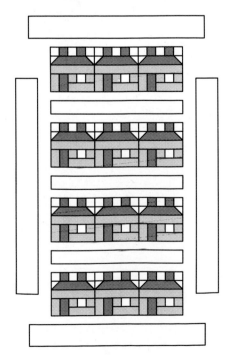

Quilt Finishing

1. Layer the quilt top with batting and backing; baste.
2. Quilt as desired.

Suggestion

Quilt in an overall pattern, such as the "Fan" (page 79), or quilt in-the-ditch of each block and quilt in a single row 1¼" from the border seam.

3. Bind the edges of the quilt.
4. Tea dye if desired.
5. Press the quilt.

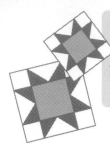

Try this traditional favorite in a little size. Vary the fabrics slightly within the block to create a scrappy look.

Country Christmas

Quilt Size: 23" x 23"

Country Christmas *by Little Quilts, 1993, Marietta, Georgia, 23" x 23". Magic stars and cheerful checks make this quilt a year-round winner. (Collection of Little Quilts)*

Star Block
Finished Block Size: 5"
1¾"-wide strips
Templates: J, K, L, M

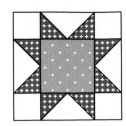

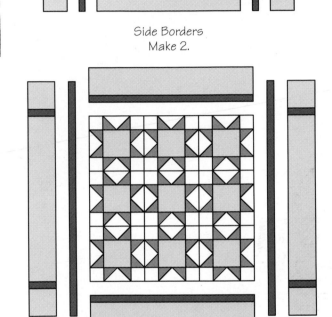

Side Borders
Make 2.

Materials
44"-wide fabric

Assorted fabric strips, each 1¾" wide
Small pieces of 9 assorted fabrics for
    center square of stars
¼ yd. green for border
½ yd. red-checked fabric for border
¼ yd. binding
¾ yd. backing

Block Cutting and Assembly

Use an assortment of 1¾"-wide strips to make 9 Star blocks as shown on page 18. You will need to cut a total of:

    36 light squares, each 1¾" x 1¾", for
        background corners

    36 light rectangles, each 1¾" x 3", for
        background of star points

    72 dark squares, each 1¾" x 1¾", for star
        points

    9 assorted squares, each 3" x 3", for center
        square of stars

Quilt Top Assembly

1. Arrange blocks in a pleasing balance of colors and prints.
2. Sew blocks into 3 rows of 3 blocks each. Press seams of alternating rows in opposite directions.
3. Sew the rows together, making sure to match the seams between each block.
4. From green fabric, cut:
    2 strips, each 1¼" x 15½"
    2 strips, each 1¼" x 23"
    4 strips, each 1¼" x 3½"
   From red-checked fabric, cut:
    4 strips, each 3½" x 15½"
    4 squares, each 3½" x 3½" (Template FF)

5. Sew the 15½" green border strips to the top and bottom of the quilt top. Sew 2 of the 15½" red-checked border strips to the top and bottom of the quilt top.
6. Sew the 23" green border strips to the sides of the quilt top.
7. Sew a 1¼" x 3½" strip of green to each end of the remaining red-checked strips; then sew a 3½" red-checked square to each end of the border as shown. Sew the pieced border to the sides of the quilt top.

Quilt Finishing

1. Layer the quilt top with batting and backing; baste.
2. Quilt as desired.

Suggestion

Quilt the border with an X, spacing to align with blocks and allowing for the binding area.

3. Bind the edges of the quilt.
4. Tea dye if desired.
5. Press the quilt.

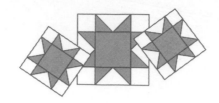

Stars in the Snow

Quilt Size: 15½" x 20½"

Stars in the Snow *by Little Quilts, 1989, Marietta, Georgia, 15½" x 20½".*
Six little stars shine through the falling snow. (Collection of Little Quilts)

Star Block
Finished Block Size: 5"
Templates: J, K, L, M

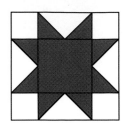

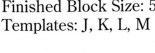

Materials
44"-wide fabric

½ yd. muslin for blocks and border
⅓ yd. red solid for stars
¼ yd. green for binding
¾ yd. backing

Block Cutting and Assembly

⭐ ⭐ ☆ **Note** ☆

The construction of this quilt has been simplified. For this reason, the quilt plan on this page does not exactly match the quilt in the photo.

1. Make 6 Star blocks as shown on page 18. You will need to cut a total of:
   24 muslin squares, each 1¾" x 1¾", for background corners
   24 muslin rectangles, each 1¾" x 3", for background of star points
   48 red squares, each 1¾" x 1¾", for star points
   6 red squares, each 3" x 3", for center square of stars
2. Sew the Star blocks into 3 rows of 2 blocks each. Press the seams of alternating rows in opposite directions.
3. Sew rows together, making sure to match the seams between each block.

4. From muslin, cut 4 border strips, each 3" x 15½"; sew to the sides first, then to the top and bottom of the quilt top.

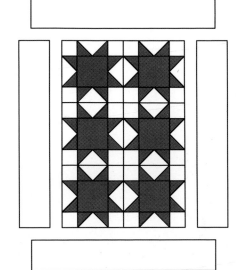

Quilt Finishing

1. Layer the quilt top with batting and backing; baste.
2. Quilt as desired.

🧵 **Suggestion**
Quilt in-the-ditch of each star and quilt a 1" diagonal grid in the border.

3. Bind the edges of the quilt.
4. Tea dye if desired.
5. Press the quilt.

Harvest Stars

Quilt Size: 24" x 24"

Harvest Stars *by Little Quilts, 1993, Marietta, Georgia, 24" x 24". Stars turned on point and checks cut on the bias give this quilt a warm, comfortable look—it looks great on a wall near a basket. Quilted by Janet Rawls. (Collection of Little Quilts)*

Star Block
Finished Block Size: 5"
1¾"-wide strips
Templates: J, K, L, M

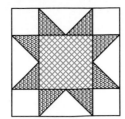

Framed Ninepatch Block
Finished Block Size: 5"
1½"-wide strips
Templates: D, F

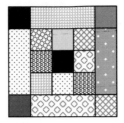

Materials
44"-wide fabric

Assorted strips, each 1¾" wide
Assorted strips, each 1½" wide
¼ yd. brown checked fabric for side
  triangles
¼ yd. brown print for side and corner
  triangles
⅓ yd. border and binding
¾ yd. backing

Block Cutting and Assembly

1. Use an assortment of 1¾"-wide strips to make 9 Star blocks as shown on page 18. You will need to cut a total of:
   36 light squares, each 1¾" x 1¾", for background corners
   36 light rectangles, each 1¾" x 3", for background of star points
   72 dark squares, each 1¾" x 1¾", for star points
   9 assorted squares, each 3" x 3", for center square of stars
2. Use an assortment of 1½"-wide strips to make 4 Ninepatch blocks as shown on page 17.
3. Frame the Ninepatch blocks. From assorted 1½"-wide strips, cut 16 strips, each 1½" x 3½", and 16 squares, each 1½" x 1½". Sew 1½" x 3½" strips to opposite sides of a Ninepatch block. Sew a 1½" square to each end of the remaining 1½" x 3½" strips and attach to the top and bottom of the block as shown.

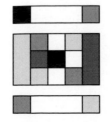

Quilt Top Assembly

 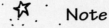

Note

The brown checked fabric in the side triangles was cut so that the check is at right angles to the Star blocks for greater design interest. To do this, you must cut the triangle so that the bias edge of the triangle is on the outside of the quilt. Normally, placing bias edges on the outer edges of a quilt is not desirable because they tend to stretch slightly unless handled very carefully.

1. If you are using a plaid or checked fabric and want it to look like the brown checked fabric in the quilt photo, cut 2 squares, each 5⅞" x 5⅞", and cut once diagonally to yield 4 side triangles. Handle the bias edges of the triangles carefully to avoid stretching.

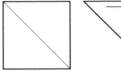

   If you are not using a directional fabric that needs to be oriented in a certain way, cut only 1 square, 8¼" x 8¼", and cut twice diagonally to yield 4 side triangles. The straight-grain edges of these triangles will be on the outside of the quilt and the bias edges toward the Star blocks.

2. From brown print, cut 2 squares, each 4⅜" x 4⅜"; cut once diagonally to yield 4 corner triangles.
3. Arrange the quilt on your design wall, alternating the Star blocks and Framed Ninepatch blocks as shown on page 50; place the side triangles.

4. Sew the blocks in diagonal rows as shown below. Press the seams of alternating rows in opposite directions.

5. Sew the rows together, making sure to match the seams between the blocks. Add the corner triangles last.
6. Measure the length of the quilt top through the center.

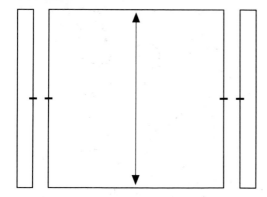

Cut 2 border strips to that measurement, each 1½" wide. Mark the center of the border strips and quilt top. Sew the border strips to the sides, matching the centers and ends and easing as necessary.

7. Measure the width of the quilt top through the center, including the side borders.

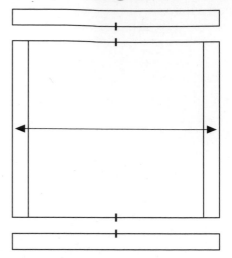

Cut 2 border strips to that measurement, each 1½" wide. Mark the center of the border strips and quilt top. Sew the border strips to the top and bottom, matching the centers and ends and easing as necessary.

Quilt Finishing

1. Layer the quilt top with batting and backing; baste.
2. Quilt as desired.

> **Suggestion**
>
> Quilt a 2" diagonal grid across the top, or quilt in-the-ditch of each block and in a single row ⅝" from the border seam.

3. Bind the edges of the quilt.
4. Tea dye if desired.
5. Press the quilt.

SUNBONNET SUE AND OVERALL BILL

Of all the Little Quilt designs, our chubby Sunbonnet Sue and Overall Bill are the most popular. These familiar figures with hidden faces tug at our heartstrings. Embellish appliqué with the buttonhole stitch.

Sunbonnet Sue Sampler

Quilt Size: 17½" x 23"

Sunbonnet Sue Sampler *by Little Quilts, 1993, Marietta, Georgia, 17½" x 23". A medley of favorite quilt blocks combine to make this sampler quilt special. Quilted by Janet Rawls. (Collection of Little Quilts)*

Sunbonnet Sue Block
Finished Block Size: 5"
Templates 1, 2, 3, 4, 5, 6, AA

House Block
Finished Block Size: 5"
1½"-wide strips
Templates: D, E, F, G, H, I

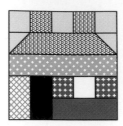

Star Block
Finished Block Size: 5"
1¾"-wide strips
Templates: J, K, L, M

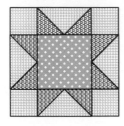

Log Cabin with Four Patch
Finished Block Size: 5"
1¼"-wide strips for Log Cabin
1½"-wide strips for center
    Four Patch
Templates: D, V, W, X, Y, Z

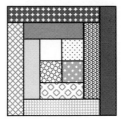

Materials
44"-wide fabric

Assorted strips in 1¼", 1½", and 1¾"
    widths
Assorted fabrics in small amounts for
    appliqué, star center, and borders
¼ yd. background for Sunbonnet Sue
    blocks
⅛ yd. black print for borders
⅛ yd. black solid for sashing
¼ yd. binding
¾ yd. backing
Black embroidery floss
Assorted small buttons for embellish-
    ment

Block Cutting and Assembly

1. From background fabric, cut 3 squares, each 5½" x 5½".
2. From assorted fabrics, cut 3 each of Templates 1, 2, 3, 4, 5, and 6.
3. Place the background square over the placement guide to help position the Sunbonnet Sue pieces. Pin the pieces in place.
4. Appliqué Sunbonnet Sue (by hand or machine) on the background square in numerical sequence. Use a buttonhole stitch to embellish the appliqué.
5. Use assorted 1½"-wide strips to make 1 House block as shown on page 19.
6. Use assorted 1¾"-wide strips to make 1 Star block as shown on page 18.
7. Use assorted 1½"-wide strips to make 1 Four Patch block as shown on page 17.
8. Make 1 Log Cabin block, using the Four Patch block made above as the center. Add 2 rows of 1¼"-wide strips around the Four Patch to complete the Log Cabin. See page 18 for Log Cabin piecing directions.

Quilt Top Assembly

1. From black solid, cut:
   3 strips, each 1½" x 5½", for vertical sashing between blocks
   2 strips, each 1½" x 11½", for horizontal sashing between rows
2. Arrange the quilt blocks and sashing as shown on page 55.
3. Sew the blocks and 5½" sashing strips together in horizontal rows.
4. Sew the rows together with 11½" sashing strips between each row.
5. For inner border, cut 2 strips, each 1½" x 11½", from black print; sew to top and bottom of quilt top. Then cut 2 strips, each 1½" x 19½"; sew to the sides of the quilt top.
6. For pieced outer border, cut assorted pieces of fabric 2½" wide in random lengths. Sew them together to create one continuous 2½"-wide strip, approximately 75" long. Cut 2 strips the length of the quilt top and sew to the sides of the quilt top. Cut 2 strips the

width of the quilt top, including the side borders, and sew to the top and bottom of the quilt top. Vary the lengths and arrange colors around the quilt.

Quilt Finishing

1. Layer the quilt top with batting and backing; baste.
2. Quilt as desired.

> ### Suggestion
> Quilt blocks in-the-ditch and around the appliqué. Quilt a row down the middle of the sashing strips and in the first border. Quilt an X on each piece of the outer border.

3. Bind the edges of the quilt.
4. Tea dye if desired.
5. Press the quilt.
6. Embellish with assorted buttons.

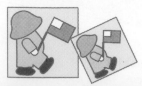

Follow the Leader

Quilt Size: 21½" x 26½"

Follow the Leader *by Little Quilts, 1993, Marietta, Georgia, 21½" x 26½". Made especially for little boys—because between the three of us, we have six—this quilt brings back memories of when ours were small. Quilted by Janet Rawls. (Collection of Little Quilts)*

Overall Bill Block
Finished Block Size: 5"
Templates 1, 2, 3, 4, 5, 6,
　　7, AA

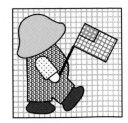

Framed Ninepatch Block
Finished Block Size: 5"
1½"-wide strips
Templates: D, F

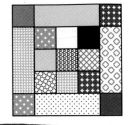

Materials
44"-wide fabric

Assorted strips, each 1½" wide
Assorted small pieces of fabric for
　　appliqué design
¼ yd. background
½ yd. border
¼ yd. binding
1 yd. backing

Block Cutting and Assembly

1. From background fabric, cut 6 squares, each 5½" x 5½".
2. From assorted fabrics, cut 6 each of Templates 2, 3, 4, 5; cut 12 of Template 1; and 3 each of Templates 6 and 7.
3. Place the background square over the placement guide to help position the Overall Bill pieces. Pin the pieces in place.
4. Appliqué Overall Bill (by hand or machine) on the background square in numerical sequence. Only 3 of the Overall Bill blocks have flags. Use a buttonhole stitch to embellish the appliqué.
5. Use assorted 1½"-wide strips to make 6 Ninepatch blocks as shown on page 17.
6. Frame the Ninepatch blocks. From assorted 1½"-wide strips, cut 24 strips, each 1½" x 3½, and 24 squares, each 1½" x 1½". Sew 1½" x 3½" strips to opposite sides of a Ninepatch block. Sew a 1½" x 1½" square to each end of the remaining 1½" x 3½" strips and attach to the top and bottom of the block as shown.

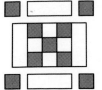

Quilt Top Assembly

1. Arrange the blocks as shown below. Sew the blocks together and press the seams of alternating rows in opposite directions.
2. Sew the rows together, making sure to match the seams between each block.
3. From border fabric, cut 2 strips, each 3½" x 20½"; sew to the sides of the quilt top.
4. Use an assortment of 1½"-wide strips to make 4 Ninepatch blocks as shown on page 17.
5. From border fabric, cut 2 strips, each 3½" x 15½". Sew a Ninepatch block to each end of the border strips; attach to top and bottom of quilt top.

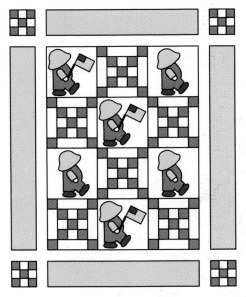

Quilt Finishing

1. Layer the quilt top with batting and backing; baste.
2. Quilt as desired.

Suggestion
Quilt around each Overall Bill and in-the-ditch of the squares. Quilt an X across the Ninepatch block. Quilt the border with an X, aligning the X with the corner of each block.

3. Bind the edges of the quilt.
4. Tea dye if desired.
5. Press the quilt.

FLAGS

Making a quilted flag is easy and fun. Change the corner block and use a variety of fabrics. Cut strips on the lengthwise grain if possible.

I Love Flags

Quilt Size: 20½" x 25½"

I Love Flags by Little Quilts, 1990, Marietta, Georgia, 20½" x 25½".
Make a flag for everyone on your gift list. Betsy would be proud!

Small Heart Block
Finished Block Size: 3½"
Templates: B, C

Materials
44"-wide fabric

½ yd. navy solid for heart background and binding
¾ yd. muslin for stripes and hearts
¾ yd. red print for stripes
1 yd. backing

Block Cutting and Assembly

Heart Block

1. From navy fabric, cut 9 squares, each 4" x 4" (Template C).
2. From muslin, cut 9 hearts (Template B).
3. Finger press the muslin square in half for a placement guide.
4. Center the heart on the muslin square and pin to hold in place.
5. Clip the V of the heart. Appliqué hearts to the navy squares.
6. Cut the navy fabric from the back of the muslin heart. Proceed carefully and use small, sharp scissors. Pull apart the heart and the navy fabric and make a small cut in the navy fabric. Insert your scissors and clip away the navy to within ⅛" of the stitching line as shown.

Back of fabric

Quilt Top Assembly

1. Sew the Heart blocks together in 3 rows of 3 hearts each. Press seams of alternating rows in opposite directions.
2. Sew the rows together, making sure to match the seams between each block.

3. For short stripes, cut 4 strips, each 2" x 15", from red print; and cut 3 strips, each 2" x 15", from muslin. Beginning with a red stripe, sew the red and muslin strips together as shown. Press seams toward the red fabric.
4. Sew heart section to short stripe section.
5. For long stripes, cut 3 strips, each 2" x 25½", from red print; and cut 3 strips, each 2" x 25½", from muslin. Beginning with a muslin strip, sew the muslin and red strips together as shown. Press seams toward red strips. Sew the long stripe section to the top section.

Quilt Finishing

1. Make a template of the large "wave" design on page 79. Start at the top. Beginning at the edge of a stripe, place the straight edge of the template on the seam. Mark the wave pattern on each stripe, placing the template end to end across the stripe. On the last stripe, place the template ¼" away from the bottom to allow for binding. Line up the waves on the short stripes with the waves on the long stripes.
2. Layer the quilt top with batting and backing; baste.
3. Quilt as desired.

Suggestion

Quilt around each heart and in-the-ditch of the navy squares. Quilt the waves on the stripes.

4. Bind the edges of the quilt.
5. Tea dye if desired.
6. Press the quilt.

Celebration Flags

Quilt Size: 13½" x 18"

Celebration Flag *by Little Quilts, 1993, Marietta, Georgia, 13½" x 18". Hang these little flags on the wall, place them on a table, or use as place mats for patriotic occasions. Quilted by Janet Rawls. (Collection of Little Quilts)*

Celebration Flag, *by Little Quilts, 1993, Marietta, Georgia, 13½" x 18". Hang this easy-to-make flag on the front door to welcome guests. Quilted by Janet Rawls. (Collection of Little Quilts)*

House Block
Finished Block Size: 5"
1½"-wide strips
Templates: D, E, F, G, H, I

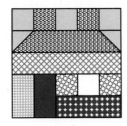

OR

Star Block
Finished Block Size: 5"
1¾"-wide strips
Templates: J, K, L, M

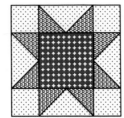

Materials
44"-wide fabric

Assorted strips, 1½" wide for House
and 1¾" wide for Star
4 assorted red strips, each 1½" x 11"
3 assorted tan strips, each 1½" x 11"
3 assorted red strips, each 1½" x 18"
3 assorted tan strips, each 1½" x 18"
1 square, 3" x 3", for Star
⅛ yd. binding
⅝ yd. backing

Block Cutting and Assembly

1. Make 1 House Block, using 1½"-wide strips
   as shown on page 19;
   OR
   make 1 Star block, using 1¾"-wide strips as
   shown on page 18.
2. To frame the blocks, select 4 different 1½"-
   wide green strips for the House block;
   OR
   select 1½"-wide gold strips for the Star block.
3. From selected strips for framing, cut 2 strips,
   each 1½" x 5½", and sew to the top and
   bottom of the block. Cut 2 strips, each 1½" x
   7½", and sew to the sides of the block.

Quilt Top Assembly

1. For short stripes: Beginning with a red strip,
   sew the 1½" x 11" red and tan strips together as shown. Press the seams toward
   the red strips.

2. Sew the short stripe section to the House or
   Star block.
3. For long stripes: Beginning with a tan strip,
   sew the 1½" x 18" tan and red strips together
   as shown. Press the seams toward the red
   strips.
4. Sew the long stripe section to the top section of
   the flag.

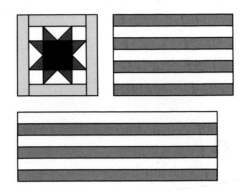

Quilt Finishing

1. Make a template of the small "wave" design
   on page 79. Start at the top. Beginning at the
   edge of a stripe, place the straight edge of
   the template on the seam. Mark the wave
   pattern on each stripe, placing the template
   end to end across the stripe. On the last
   stripe, place the template ¼" away from the
   bottom to allow for binding. Line up the
   waves on the short stripes with the waves on
   the long stripes.
2. Layer the quilt top with batting and backing;
   baste.
3. Quilt as desired.

Suggestion
Quilt the corner block as desired, or
simply in-the-ditch and around the border. Quilt the "waves" on the stripes.

4. Bind the edges of the quilt.
5. Tea dye if desired.
6. Press the quilt.

My Best Bows

Quilt Size: 24" x 24"

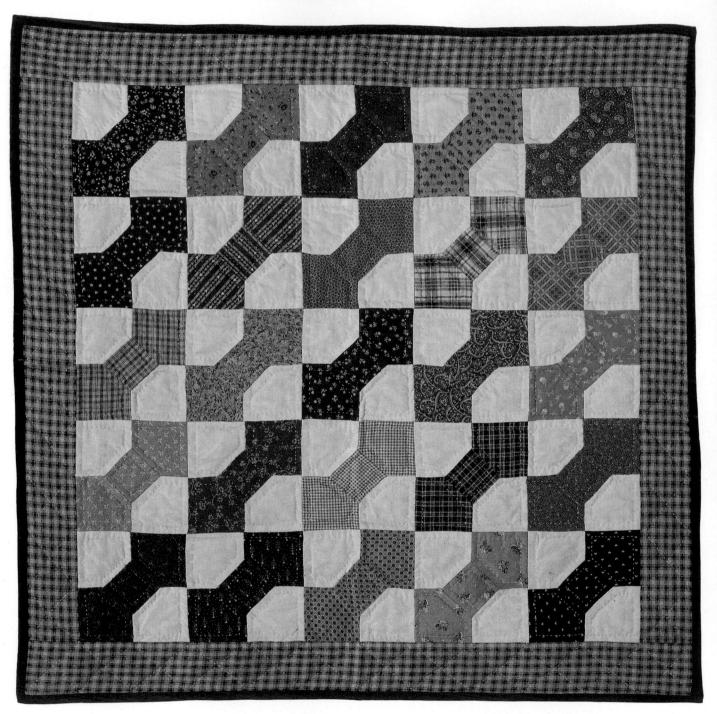

My Best Bows by Little Quilts, 1989, Marietta, Georgia, 24" x 24". Pick your favorite fabrics and make this wonderful quilt—use to decorate anywhere! (Collection of Little Quilts)

Bow Tie Block
Finished Block Size: 4"
Templates: BB, CC

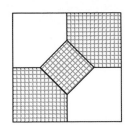

Materials
44"-wide fabric

½ yd. muslin
25 assorted fabrics, approximately
   8" x 8"
½ yd. fabric for borders and binding
1 yd. backing

Block Cutting and Assembly

1. From muslin, cut 50 of Template BB.
2. For each Bow Tie block, cut 2 of Template BB, and 1 of Template CC from the same fabric. To make 25 Bow Tie blocks, you will need a total of 50 of Template BB and 25 of Template CC.
3. Assemble 25 Bow Tie blocks as shown in the piecing diagram below, matching the fabrics of the bow tie pieces for each block.

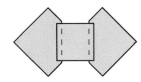

Start and stop stitching
¼" from edges of square.
Backstitch at each end.

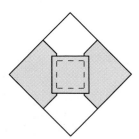

Stitch background
to remaining sides
of square, between
previous seams.

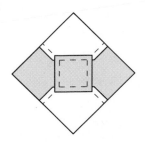

Stitch 4 remaining seams
from backstitch spot
to outer edge.

Quilt Top Assembly

1. Arrange blocks as shown below. Sew blocks together in 5 rows of 5 blocks each. Press the seams of alternating rows in opposite directions.
2. Sew the rows together, making sure to match the seams between each block.
3. From border fabric, cut 2 strips, each 2½" x 20½", and sew to the sides of the quilt top.
4. Cut 2 strips, each 2½" x 24½", and sew to the top and bottom of the quilt top.

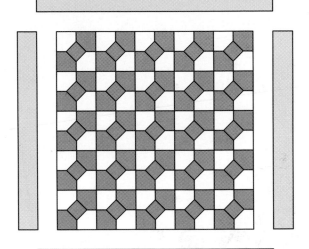

Quilt Finishing

1. Layer the quilt top with batting and backing; baste.
2. Quilt as desired.

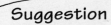

Suggestion

Quilt ¼" inside each section of the bow tie. Quilt a 1¼" diagonal grid in the borders.

3. Bind the edges of the quilt.
4. Tea dye if desired.
5. Press the quilt.

Homecoming Wreath

Quilt Size: 21" x 21"

Homecoming Wreath *by Little Quilts, 1989, Marietta, Georgia, 21" x 21". All hearts come home for Christmas, and this quilt symbolizes the feeling.*

Wreath Block
Finished Block Size: 7"
Templates: 1, 2, 3, 4, EE

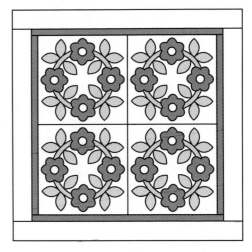

Materials
44"-wide fabric

¾ yd. background fabric
⅛ yd. each of 4 assorted green fabrics for leaves and stems
¼ yd. each of 4 assorted red fabrics for flowers and sawtooth border
Small amount of muslin for flower center
½ yd. red fabric for inner border and binding
¾ yd. backing

Block Cutting and Assembly

1. From background fabric, cut 4 squares, each 7½" x 7½" (Template EE).
2. From each of the 4 green fabrics, cut:
   4 of Template 1 (16 total)
   12 of Template 2 (48 total)
3. From each of the 4 assorted red fabrics, cut 4 of Template 3 (16 total).
4. From muslin, cut 16 of Template 4.
5. Place the background square over the placement guide to help position the stems, leaves, and flowers. Pin the pieces in place.
6. Appliqué the wreaths to the background squares in numerical sequence.

Quilt Top Assembly

1. Join the 4 blocks together as shown on this page.
2. For inner border, cut 2 strips, each 1" x 14½", from red fabric; sew to the sides of the quilt top. Then cut 2 strips, each 1" x 15½", and sew to the top and bottom of the quilt top.
3. For middle border, cut 2 strips, each 2" x 15½", from background fabric; sew to the sides of the quilt top. Then cut 2 strips, each 2" x 18½"; sew to the top and bottom of the quilt top.

4. For sawtooth border, use an assortment of red prints and the background print to make 52 half-square triangle units. You will need to cut a total of:
   26 squares, each 2⅜" x 2⅜", from red prints
   26 squares, each 2⅜" x 2⅜", from background print
Cut each of the squares once diagonally and assemble triangles as shown.

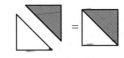

5. Sew 12 half-square triangle units together to make 4 pieced border strips as shown.

Make 4.

6. Sew a pieced border strip to each side of the quilt top.

7. Sew a half-square triangle unit to each end of the remaining pieced borders as shown; sew to the top and bottom of the quilt top.

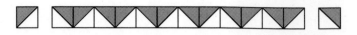

Quilt Finishing

1. Layer the quilt top with batting and backing; baste.
2. Quilt as desired.

Suggestion

Quilt around each of the appliqué shapes and in-the-ditch of the blocks and first narrow border. Using the sawtooth border as a guide, quilt a diagonal grid in the borders.

3. Bind the edges of the quilt.
4. Tea dye if desired.
5. Press the quilt.

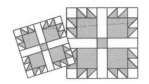

Here's to the Bears

Quilt Size: 31½" x 44½"

A TRIBUTE TO OUR BEARS

This scrap quilt combines many of the blocks used in this book and features a Bear's Paw block in the center, especially for our bears. We love bears—they love Little Quilts, and these bears have been patient with us over the years, sitting very still for pictures, riding upside down across country in shipping cartons, and being on their best behavior at Quilt Market. This is an opportunity for you to use any leftover blocks. (Quilted by Janet Rawls.) Enjoy!

1 Bear's Paw Block:
Finished Block Size: 7"
Templates: D, F, HH, I

5 Heart Blocks
Finished Block Size: 4"
Templates: A, DD

3 Star Blocks
Finished Block Size: 5"
Templates: J, K, L, M

2 Log Cabin Blocks with Four
    Patch Centers
Finished Block Size: 5"
Templates: D, V, W, X, Y, Z

2 Courthouse Steps Blocks with
    Four Patch Centers
Finished Block Size: 5"
Templates: D, V, X, Z

2 Log Cabin Blocks with Half-
    Square Triangle Centers
Finished Block Size: 5"
Templates: N, V, W, X, Y, Z

1 Courthouse Steps Block with
    Half-Square Triangle Center
Finished Block Size: 5"
Templates: N, V, X, Z

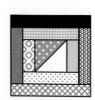

2 House Blocks
Finished Block Size: 5"
Templates: D, E, F, G, H, I

38 Four Patch Blocks
Finished Block Size: 2"
Template: D

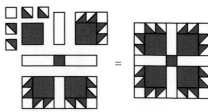

Materials
44"-wide fabric

Assorted scraps of blue, tan, red, green, and gold
Assorted strips in 1¼", 1½", and 1¾" widths
5 assorted tan squares, each 4½" x 4½"
⅛ yd. each of 2 brown fabrics for inner border
½ yd. assorted red and brown fabrics for pieced outer border
2 strips, each 1¾" x 20½", in brown or black for sashing between rows
¼ yd. brown for binding
1⅓ yds. backing
Black embroidery floss
Assorted old buttons for embellishment

Bear's Paw Block Cutting and Assembly

1. Make 1 Bear's Paw block for the center. From assorted tan fabrics, cut a total of:
    4 of Template D
    4 of Template F
    16 of Template I
   From assorted blue fabrics, cut a total of:
    1 of Template D
    4 of Template HH
    16 of Template I

2. Sew blue and tan triangles to make 16 half-square triangle units as shown.

3. Assemble the Bear's Paw block (by hand or machine) as shown in the piecing diagram below.

4. Cut 2 strips, each 1" x 7½", from brown fabric and sew to the sides of the block; then cut 2 strips, each 1" x 8½", and sew to the top and bottom of the block. Press the seams toward the border.

Center Section Assembly

1. Use an assortment of 1½"-wide strips to make 38 Four Patch blocks as shown on page 17.
2. From a variety of blue fabrics, cut a total of 6 squares, each 2½" x 2½" (Template HH).
3. Arrange the Four Patch blocks and squares around the Bear's Paw block as shown below to create a pleasing balance of color.
4. Sew the 4 blocks above and below the Bear's Paw block together; attach to the top and bottom of the framed block.
5. Sew the remainder of the blocks together to make 12 rows of 3 blocks each. Sew 6 rows together and attach to the right side of the framed block. Sew 6 rows together and attach to the left side of the framed block.
6. Sew the 2 brown or black 1¾" x 20½" strips to top and bottom of center section.

Block Cutting and Assembly

1. Heart Blocks: Cut 5 hearts (Template A) from assorted fabrics. Using black embroidery floss, appliqué hearts with a buttonhole stitch to the 5 assorted tan squares, each 4½" x 4½" (Template DD). Sew the Heart blocks together. Sew the row of Heart blocks to the top of the center section.
2. Four Patch Blocks: Use an assortment of 1½"-wide strips to make 4 Four Patch blocks as shown on page 17. These will be used in the Log Cabin and Courthouse Steps blocks.

3. Half-Square Triangles: Cut 6 of Template N from assorted scraps and assemble 3 half-square triangles as shown. These will be used in the Log Cabin and Court-house Steps blocks.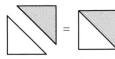
4. Log Cabin Blocks: Use an assortment of 1¼"-wide strips to make 4 Log Cabin blocks. Begin 3 blocks with a Four Patch, and 1 block with a half-square triangle unit. Add 2 rows of strips around the center unit. See page 18 for Log Cabin piecing directions, substituting center units for center square.

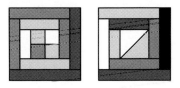

5. Courthouse Steps Blocks: Use an assortment of 1¼"-wide strips to make 4 Courthouse Steps blocks. Begin 1 block with a half-square triangle unit, and 2 blocks with a Four Patch. Add strips to opposite sides of the center unit as shown.

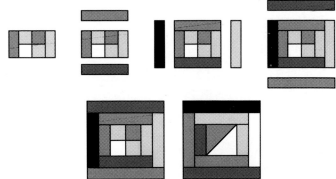

6. Use an assortment of 1¾"-wide strips to make 3 Star blocks as shown on page 18.
7. Use an assortment of 1½"-wide strips to make 2 House blocks as shown on page 19.
8. For the top row, join 1 Star block, 1 Log Cabin block, and 2 Courthouse Steps blocks as shown on page 70. Sew to the top of the center section, above the row of Heart blocks.
9. For the last 2 rows, join remaining House, Star, Log Cabin, and Courthouse Steps blocks as shown. Sew rows to bottom of the center section.

10. For inner border, cut 2 strips, each 2" x 34", from brown fabric; sew to the sides of the quilt top. From second brown fabric, cut 2 strips, each 1¾" x 23½", and sew to the top and bottom of the quilt top.

Pieced Outer Border

The outer border for this quilt is made by combining Bow Tie blocks with random lengths of red and brown strips of fabric.

1. From assorted red prints, cut a total of:
    24 of Template BB for bow tie and background
    6 of Template CC for bow tie knot
    From assorted brown prints, cut a total of:
    24 of Template BB for bow tie and background
    6 of Template CC for bow tie knot
2. Assemble 12 Bow Tie blocks as shown in the piecing diagram on page 63. Make 6 red bow ties with brown backgrounds, and 6 brown bow ties with red backgrounds.
3. From assorted red and brown fabrics, cut 4½"-wide strips in various lengths.
4. Arrange Bow Tie blocks and lengths of red and brown strips around the quilt top as shown in the quilt plan, top right.
5. For side borders, sew blocks and strips together, adjusting the lengths of the red and

brown strips to make 2 border strips, each 36½" long; attach to sides of the quilt top.
6. For top and bottom borders, sew blocks and strips together, adjusting lengths of red and brown strips to make 2 border strips, each 31½" long; attach to top and bottom of the quilt top.

Quilt Finishing

1. Layer quilt with batting and backing; baste.
2. Quilt each block as desired.

> ### Suggestion
> Quilt a diagonal grid across the center section and through the Four Patch blocks. Quilt a single row down the middle of the sashing. Quilt in-the-ditch of the Bow Tie blocks. Using the heart (Template A), randomly place and mark hearts in the border; quilt.

3. Bind the edges of the quilt.
4. Tea dye if desired.
5. Press the quilt.
6. Embellish with old buttons.

Little Pillows

Pillow Size: 5" to 9"

These pillows are the perfect companion for your Little Quilt! Make lots of these tiny pillows and fill a basket, place them on a shelf, or give small furniture a cozy look. Use any leftover blocks and precut strips from your baskets and have fun.

Little Pillows by Little Quilts, 1993, Marietta, Georgia, 5"–9". Make this collection of tiny pillows to coordinate with your Little Quilts. Fill a basket or use them with small furniture. Quilted and finished by Jeannine Hartman.

Materials
44"-wide fabric

1 Little Quilt block
Assorted 1½"-wide strips for borders
Square of muslin for backing quilt block (1" larger than block)
Square of fabric for pillow back (1" larger than top)
Backing, batting, and thread to match
Old buttons if desired

Assembly

1. Choose one of the following ideas to complete your pillow top.

   ❤ Frame the block with precut 1½"-wide strips. Sew to the sides first, then to the top and bottom.
   ❤ Frame the block "Log Cabin" style. See page 18.
   ❤ Add a 1¼"-wide framing strip, then add a 2" border. Remember, add strips to the sides first, then to the top and bottom.
   ❤ Make the pillow without framing the quilt block.

2. Cut batting and a piece of muslin slightly larger than the pillow top. Layer backing, batting, and pillow top together; baste.

3. Quilt the pillow top as desired. Simple quilting is sufficient.

4. Sew a row of basting around the edges of the quilted pillow top to hold the layers together when sewing the front to the back.

5. Sew any buttons on at this time if desired.

6. Place the pillow top and back together with right sides together. Sew around the edges, using a ¼"-wide seam and leaving a small 2" opening for stuffing. Turn right side out; stuff firmly and blindstitch the opening.

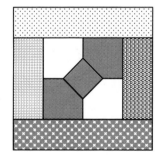 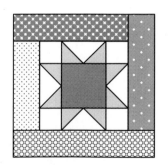  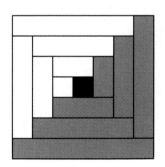

¼" seam allowance

DD
Heart Background
Here's to the Bears

4"

← straight of grain →

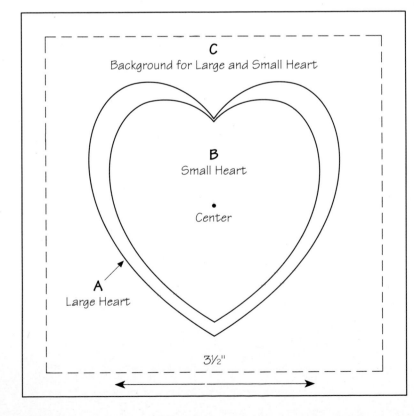

C
Background for Large and Small Heart

B
Small Heart

Center

A
Large Heart

3½"

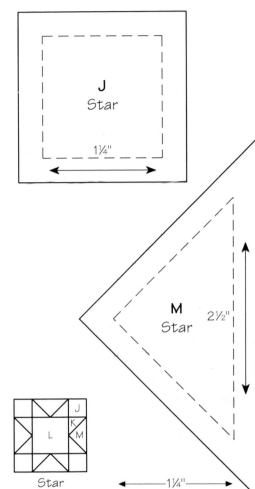

J
Star

1¼"

M
Star

2½"

Star
Template Placement

J
K
M
L

1¼"

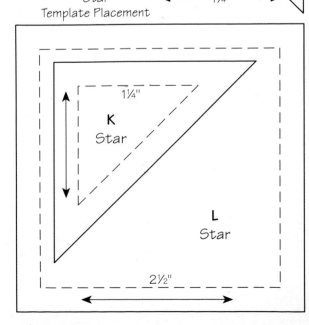

1¼"

K
Star

L
Star

2½"

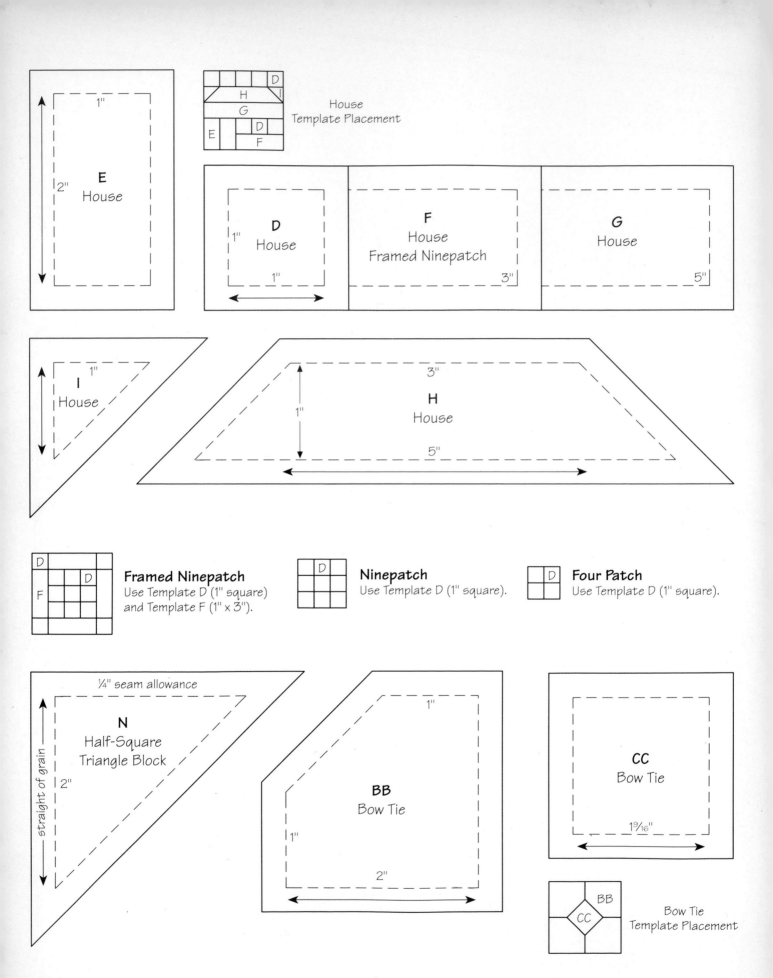

E
House

2"
1"

House
Template Placement

D
House
1"
1"

F
House
Framed Ninepatch
3"

G
House
5"

I
House
1"

H
House
3"
1"
5"

Framed Ninepatch
Use Template D (1" square)
and Template F (1" x 3").

Ninepatch
Use Template D (1" square).

Four Patch
Use Template D (1" square).

¼" seam allowance

N
Half-Square
Triangle Block
straight of grain
2"

BB
Bow Tie
1"
1"
2"

CC
Bow Tie
1 9⁄16"

Bow Tie
Template Placement

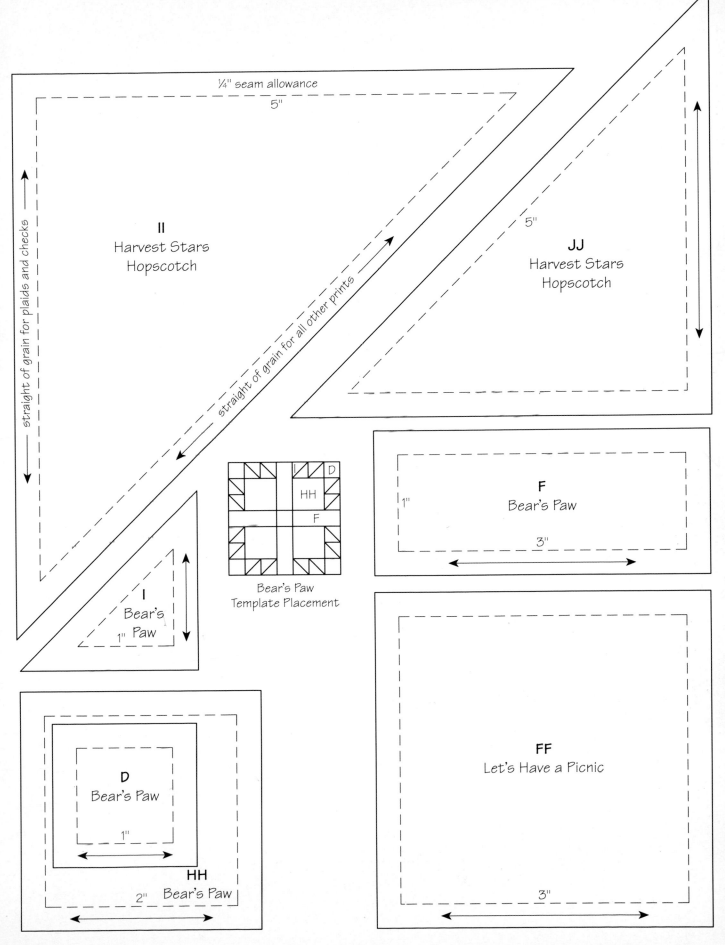

¼" seam allowance

5"

II
Harvest Stars
Hopscotch

straight of grain for plaids and checks

straight of grain for all other prints

5"

JJ
Harvest Stars
Hopscotch

Bear's Paw
Template Placement

I
Bear's
1" Paw

F
Bear's Paw

1"

3"

D
Bear's Paw

1"

HH
Bear's Paw

2"

FF
Let's Have a Picnic

3"

¼" seam allowance

EE
Background
for Wreath

2

3

4

1

7"

← straight of grain →

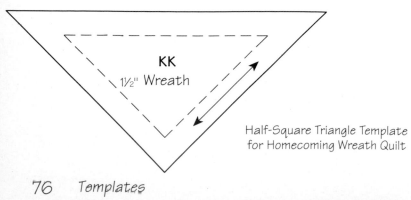

KK
1½" Wreath

Half-Square Triangle Template
for Homecoming Wreath Quilt

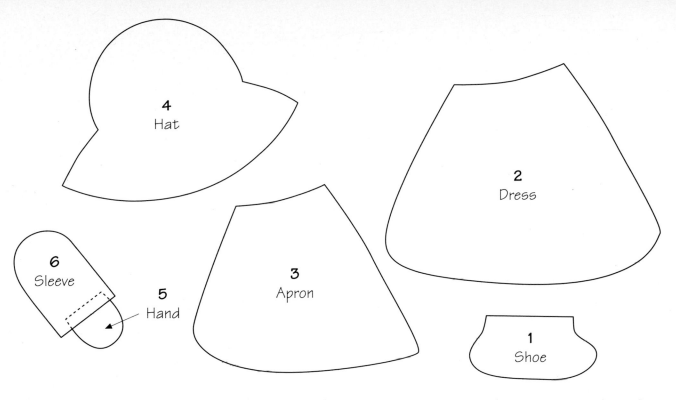

4
Hat

6
Sleeve

5
Hand

3
Apron

2
Dress

1
Shoe

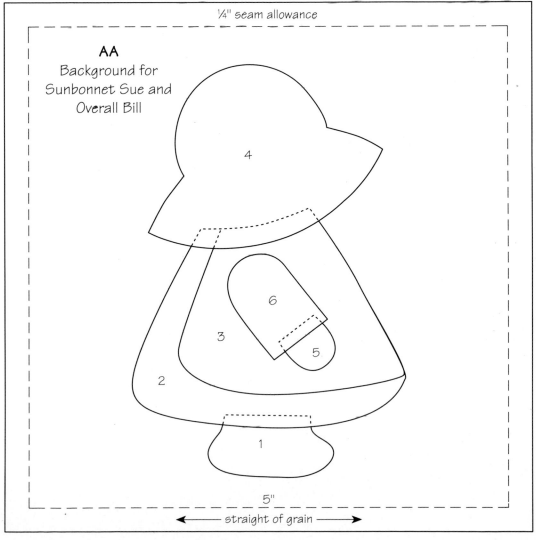

¼" seam allowance

AA
Background for
Sunbonnet Sue and
Overall Bill

4

6

3

5

2

1

5"

← straight of grain →

Note: Dotted lines on pattern indicate overlapped pieces.

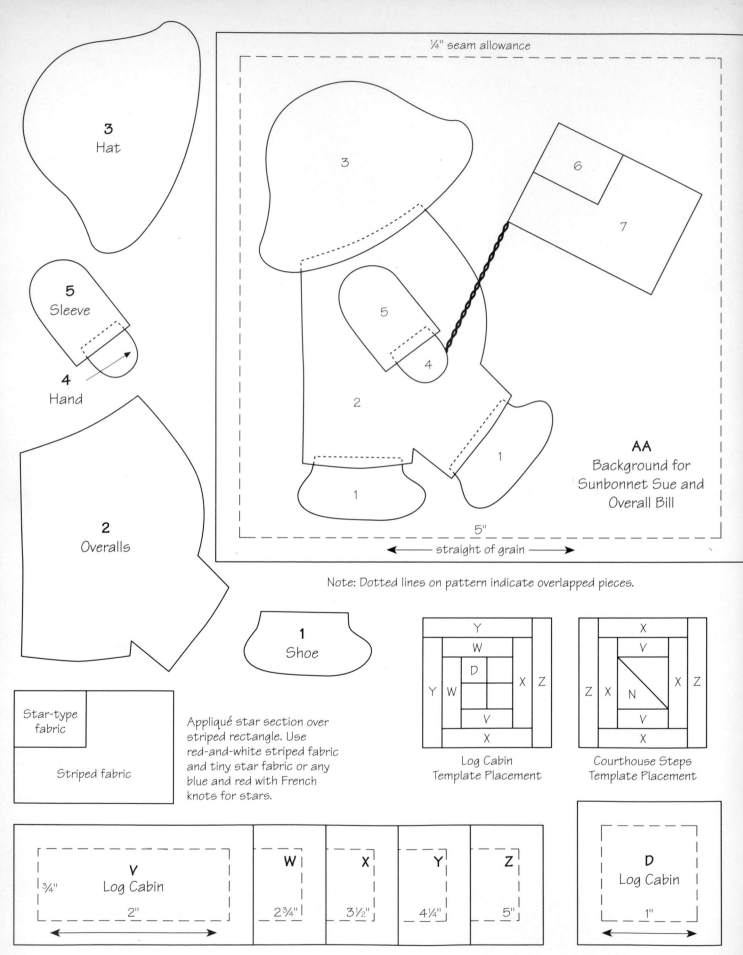

3
Hat

5
Sleeve

4
Hand

2
Overalls

¼" seam allowance

3

6

7

5

4

2

1

1

AA
Background for
Sunbonnet Sue and
Overall Bill

5"

← straight of grain →

Note: Dotted lines on pattern indicate overlapped pieces.

1
Shoe

Star-type
fabric

Striped fabric

Appliqué star section over
striped rectangle. Use
red-and-white striped fabric
and tiny star fabric or any
blue and red with French
knots for stars.

Y
W
D
Y   W   X   Z
V
X

Log Cabin
Template Placement

X
V
Z   X   N   X   Z
V
X

Courthouse Steps
Template Placement

V
Log Cabin
¾"
2"

W
2¾"

X
3½"

Y
4¼"

Z
5"

D
Log Cabin
1"

Log Cabin with Four Patch and Half-Square Triangle Center
Use Templates V, X, and Z for Courthouse Steps blocks.

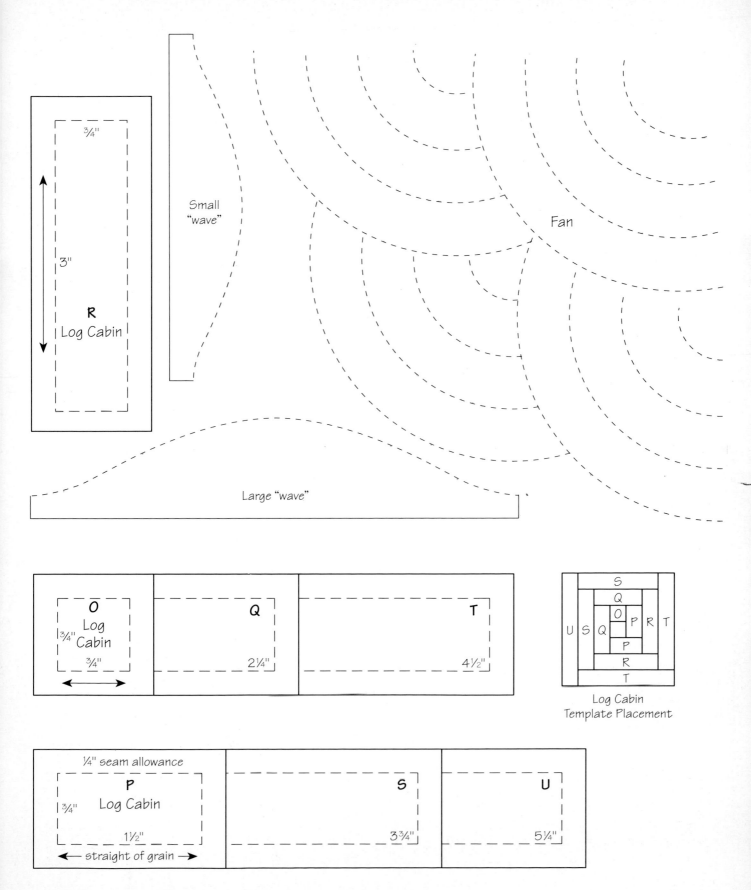

¾"

3"

R
Log Cabin

Small
"wave"

Fan

Large "wave"

O
Log
Cabin
¾"   ¾"

Q
2¼"

T
4½"

S
Q
U S Q O P R T
P
R
T

Log Cabin
Template Placement

¼" seam allowance
P
Log Cabin
¾"   1½"
◄── straight of grain ──►

S
3¾"

U
5¼"

Log Cabin Templates for Country Cabin and Feedsack Furrows

That Patchwork Place Publications and Products

BOOKS

All the Blocks Are Geese by Mary Sue Suit
Angle Antics by Mary Hickey
Animas Quilts by Jackie Robinson
Appliqué Borders: An Added Grace by Jeana Kimball
Appliquilt™: *Whimsical One-Step Appliqué* by Tonee White
Baltimore Bouquets by Mimi Dietrich
Basket Garden by Mary Hickey
Biblical Blocks by Rosemary Makhan
Blockbuster Quilts by Margaret J. Miller
Calendar Quilts by Joan Hanson
Cathedral Window: A Fresh Look by Nancy J. Martin
Corners in the Cabin by Paulette Peters
Country Medallion Sampler by Carol Doak
Country Threads by Connie Tesene and Mary Tendall
Easy Machine Paper Piecing by Carol Doak
Even More by Trudie Hughes
Fantasy Flowers: Pieced Flowers for Quilters
    by Doreen Cronkite Burbank
Feathered Star Sampler by Marsha McCloskey
Fit To Be Tied by Judy Hopkins
Five- and Seven-Patch Blocks & Quilts for the ScrapSaver™
    by Judy Hopkins
Four-Patch Blocks & Quilts for the ScrapSaver™
    by Judy Hopkins
Fun with Fat Quarters by Nancy J. Martin
Go Wild with Quilts: 14 North American Birds and Animals
    by Margaret Rolfe
Handmade Quilts by Mimi Dietrich
Happy Endings—Finishing the Edges of Your Quilt
    by Mimi Dietrich
Holiday Happenings by Christal Carter
Home for Christmas by Nancy J. Martin and Sharon Stanley
In The Beginning by Sharon Evans Yenter
Jacket Jazz by Judy Murrah
Lessons in Machine Piecing by Marsha McCloskey
Little By Little: Quilts in Miniature by Mary Hickey
Little Quilts by Alice Berg, Sylvia Johnson, and
    Mary Ellen Von Holt
Lively Little Logs by Donna McConnell
Loving Stitches: A Guide to Fine Hand Quilting
    by Jeana Kimball
More Template-Free™ *Quiltmaking* by Trudie Hughes
Nifty Ninepatches by Carolann M. Palmer
Nine-Patch Blocks & Quilts for the ScrapSaver™
    by Judy Hopkins
Not Just Quilts by Jo Parrott
On to Square Two by Marsha McCloskey
Osage County Quilt Factory by Virginia Robertson
Painless Borders by Sally Schneider
A Perfect Match: A Guide to Precise Machine Piecing
    by Donna Lynn Thomas

Picture Perfect Patchwork by Naomi Norman
Piecemakers® *Country Store* by the Piecemakers
Pineapple Passion by Nancy Smith and Lynda Milligan
A Pioneer Doll and Her Quilts by Mary Hickey
Pioneer Storybook Quilts by Mary Hickey
Quick & Easy Quiltmaking: 26 Projects Featuring Speedy
    Cutting and Piecing Methods by Mary Hickey,
    Nancy J. Martin, Marsha McCloskey & Sara Nephew
The Quilters' Companion: Everything You Need to Know to
    Make Beautiful Quilts compiled by That Patchwork Place
Quilts for All Seasons: Year-Round Log Cabin Designs
    by Christal Carter
Quilts for Baby: Easy as A, B, C by Ursula Reikes
Quilts for Kids by Carolann M. Palmer
Quilts from Nature by Joan Colvin
Quilts to Share by Janet Kime
Red and Green: An Appliqué Tradition by Jeana Kimball
Red Wagon Originals by Gerry Kimmel and Linda Brannock
Rotary Riot: 40 Fast & Fabulous Quilts by Judy Hopkins
    and Nancy J. Martin
Rotary Roundup: 40 More Fast & Fabulous Quilts by Judy
    Hopkins and Nancy J. Martin
Round About Quilts by J. Michelle Watts
Samplings from the Sea by Rosemary Makhan
Scrap Happy by Sally Schneider
Sensational Settings: Over 80 Ways to Arrange Your Quilt
    Blocks by Joan Hanson
Sewing on the Line: Fast and Easy Foundation Piecing
    by Lesly-Claire Greenberg
Shortcuts: A Concise Guide to Rotary Cutting
    by Donna Lynn Thomas (metric version available)
Small Talk by Donna Lynn Thomas
Smoothstitch™ *Quilts: Easy Machine Appliqué*
    by Roxi Eppler
The Stitchin' Post by Jean Wells and Lawry Thorn
Strips That Sizzle by Margaret J. Miller
Tea Party Time: Romantic Quilts and Tasty Tidbits
    by Nancy J. Martin
Template-Free™ *Quiltmaking* by Trudie Hughes
Template-Free™ *Quilts and Borders* by Trudie Hughes
Template-Free® *Stars* by Jo Parrott
Watercolor Quilts by Pat Maixner Magaret and
    Donna Ingram Slusser
Women and Their Quilts by Nancyann Johanson Twelker

TOOLS
6" Bias Square®	Rotary Mate™
8" Bias Square®	Rotary Rule™
Metric Bias Square®	Ruby Beholder™
BiRangle™	ScrapSaver™
Pineapple Rule	

VIDEO
Shortcuts to America's Best-Loved Quilts

Many titles are available at your local quilt shop. For more information, send $2 for a color catalog to That Patchwork Place, Inc., PO Box 118, Bothell WA 98041-0118 USA.

☎ Call 1-800-426-3126 for the name and location of the quilt shop nearest you.